KB136562

Highly Advanced Reading Curriculum

READING
EDGE

E-field Academy

Reading gives us insight into our life and helps to visualize our future.
It gives us someplace to go when we have to stay where we are. - *Mason Cooley*

We're

Table of Contents READING EDGE SMART 2

Introduction

Every student knows studying English requires a lot of patience. Even worse, some English books are difficult and boring. Fortunately, there is a way you can change your perspective on learning English. Now you can develop your reading skills in an enjoyable way.

The Reading EDGE Smart series will help you to improve your reading skills. You can learn how to read with a purpose.

Each level of this series comes with one text book, one guide book and one audio component. Each book is organized into 5 units consisting of vocabulary and related questions. One of the key features of this series is that it integrates many skills: reading, vocabulary building, listening and writing.

This series also deals with a variety of unique and interesting topics, and the readings are graded to the appropriate length and depth depending on the English proficiency level of the student.

After reading, students will be challenged to guess the meaning of words used in the passage, summarize the passage, and solve various types of questions.

Students can listen to the entire script by MP3 or use the attached CD. Students will broaden their English ability from reading to listening, speaking and writing. This integrated approach will enable students to dramatically improve their English.

We're Reading EDGE Smart Features

	READING EDGE SMART 1~2	READING EDGE SMART 3~4	READING EDGE SMART 5~6
Unit	Topic based	Korean SAT test based	In-depth reading skill based
Reading skill	Speed Reading	Impact Reading	Power Reading
	Essential skills for reading	Essential skills for preparing for the Korean SAT test	Essential skills for In-depth reading

Structure Vol.2

Reading Passages

The Reading EDGE Smart series covers a wide variety of topics ranging from teen life to social issues. This series also covers academic and contemporary topics, which will motivate students to study English. The real life topics will provide students with knowledge and an enjoyable reading experience. In addition, passages related to social issues will give them more insight into everyday life and help foster logical thinking skills. This series has longer passages, consisting of over 300 words, which will help students get used to reading longer passages clearly and confidently.

Words

Students are encouraged to read the definitions in English, which provides them greater exposure to English vocabulary. After reading the definitions in English, they are asked to translate them into Korean. This process will motivate students to think in English first, then guess the matching Korean word.

Question Types

After reading each passage, students are advised to answer questions related to the passage. These questions are meant to help students promote their English comprehension skills. In addition, they are designed for students who are preparing for various types of tests including school tests, college entrance exams and internationally recognized tests such as TOEFL. The question styles used in the Reading EDGE Smart series include multiple choice, fill in the blank and summary completion. The activities in the Reading EDGE Smart will ensure greater reading fluency and exam success. Completing the summary will contribute to improving students' writing skills by enhancing their ability to think in English.

Tips

This section provides additional information related to the passages in order to encourage further thought on the topics.

Review

This section gives students a chance to practice words and idiomatic expressions learned in each unit using various approaches.

Reading Skills Section

The Reading EDGE Smart Series takes three different approaches to developing and improving reading skills: Speed Reading, Impact Reading, and Power Reading. These sections will help students grasp the essential skills required to improve their reading ability.

Guide Book

The Reading EDGE Smart Guide Book consists of Korean translations, idiomatic expressions, structure review, grammar tips and answer keys.

What sculpture is to a block of marble, education is to a human soul.

- Joseph Addison

Unit 1

Education & Language

Read the following and answer the questions.

Dear Annie,

My daughter, Amy, is a special and bright child who also happens to be a popular actor. It's impossible for her to go to school on a daily basis because she acts in a soap opera. So, instead of going to school, I teach her at home. As you know, homeschooling is very common in the United States. Millions of families in the U.S. participate in homeschooling.

However, we live in California where it was recently decided in court that parents without proper teaching certification are no longer allowed to homeschool their children. This ruling resulted from the case of a boy who was abused by his parents during his homeschooling. I want the best education possible for Amy, and sending her to public school isn't an option for us. Can you offer any advice?

Trying to Teach, in California

Dear Trying,

Unfortunately, as a result of this new law, many Californian families are opting to move out of the State in order to continue homeschooling. But before (a) _____ (make) such a drastic decision, consider the upside to public schools. As you know, homeschooling differs greatly from studying at school. Homeschooling makes it difficult to make memories with classmates and conform to the proper academic standards.

On the other hand, it is possible to give the best education for each student's individual academic level and interest. So, if you are determined to homeschool your daughter, why not hire a private teacher to come to your home and work alongside you? That way you still have control of your daughter's education and schedule, and she can continue to pursue acting.

Good luck,

Annie

TIP

A Suitable Job For a Lady

+ In the famous English novel, *Jane Eyre*, Jane had no parents and no money, so she became a governess. A governess was a female employee who's job was to teach the children of her employer. At that time, it was one of the few decent jobs available to a lady in Jane's situation.

1. What is the purpose of the first letter?

① to ask advice about California laws
② to ask Annie to teach her daughter
③ to find a good homeschool teacher for her daughter
④ to ask advice on how to continue homeschooling her daughter
⑤ to find out more about special programs for talented children

Speed Reading

2. What is the appropriate verb form for the blank (a)?

_____

3. Write T if the statement is true. Write F if is false.

① Amy is homeschooled because her busy schedule does not suit regular school. _____

② Because of a new law, it will be harder to do homeschooling in some places. _____

③ Homeschooling has better academic standards than public school. _____

Words	Read the following definitions and translate them into Korean.

• **soap opera**: a television drama series: _____
• **proper**: correct or most suitable _____
• **certification**: qualification to do something _____
• **ruling**: an official decision made by a judge or court _____
• **case**: a crime or mystery that the police are investigating _____
• **abuse**: to cause harm to someone _____
• **conform**: to be of the required type or quality _____

Read the following and answer the questions.

These days, children are expected to know so much more before they reach kindergarten. Supporters of early education argue that it's proving to have long-term benefits for children. However, not everyone believes that early education is beneficial. Some educators feel that this type of structured syllabus is not appropriate for children under six because it is too fatiguing.

(A) Many people agree that early education is necessary and the positive effects of educating babies before birth are proven. Any concepts taught between the ages of 0 to 3 are shown to stimulate brain development. Think about Mozart. His musical talents could have been undeveloped without training at an early age from his father. Thanks to his father's guidance, Mozart was able to play the harpsichord by the time he was three years old! Early education definitely works wonders.

(B) Research shows that high-quality, developmentally-appropriate, early-childhood programs produce positive effects. Some children speak foreign languages fluently thanks to early education. However, too much education at an early age can have negative effects on children's development because of the stress. If early education is misdirected or supplied at the wrong time, it can bring ⓐ serious harm to children, such as a speech disorder or a learning disability.

Words   Read the following definitions and translate them into Korean.

• **supporter:** someone who is in favor of something or someone _____

• **long-term:** over an extended period of time _____

• **positive:** good, constructive _____

• **stimulate:** to encourage someone to do something _____

• **disorder:** a problem or illness _____

• **disability:** a physical or mental handicap _____

1. Which saying best describes writer A's opinion?

① The sooner, the better.
② Prevention is the best medicine.
③ There are two sides to every coin.
④ Look before you leap.
⑤ Slow and steady wins the race.

2. Which best describes writer B's opinion?

① Language education should begin at an early age.
② Early education is harmful to children.
③ The younger a child is, the faster he or she can learn.
④ Education should be appropriate for a child's age and development.
⑤ Parents should start early education programs.

3. What is given as an example of the underlined part ⓐ?

_____

I Want Some Rice, Not Lice!

✦ It is tricky for native Koreans to pronounce "L" and "R" correctly. Most Korean parents want their children to speak English fluently. Some of them even arrange for their children to have tongue surgery. They believe that cutting the frenulum(the tissue under the tongue) will improve their child's English pronunciation. However, many experts disagree with this theory.

Read the following and answer the questions.

Hardly anyone denies that English is the most influential language in the world. For years Spanish has been considered second rate to (a) this language. However, (b) it is gaining greater prominence as one of the fastest growing languages.

There are over 500 million Spanish-speaking people worldwide. Furthermore, Spanish is the official language of twenty-one nations; such as Argentina, Belize, Bolivia, Chile, Colombia, Cuba, Mexico, Peru, Spain, and Venezuela. In America there are over 30 million Spanish speakers. Many Hispanic people have immigrated to America over the years and their population continues to grow, making Spanish the most popular foreign language in the U.S.

Latin America's economic growth is one of the main causes of the resurgence of the language's popularity. The ability to speak Spanish is a necessity economically because of the growing Latin influence. As countries in Latin America are consolidating and expanding their economies, this language is used more frequently as a means of communication for commerce.

Religion has also ⓐ _____ (play) an important role in the growth of Spanish. The growth of the Spanish influence is as simple as the birds and the bees. That is, they are having more children than other cultures. Most Latin people are Catholic and, therefore, do not use contraception or believe in abortion. As a result, the growing population has more economic influence and power.

The influence of Latin economics and the increase in the Spanish speaking community are the main causes of this growth in popularity. Without a doubt, Spanish is set to become more and more important.

TIP

The Next America's Sweetheart?

+ In proportion to their growing population, the influence of Hispanics (people from Latin America or Spain, and their descendants) in Hollywood is increasing. In 2007, Time Magazine chose America Ferrera as one of the '100 Most Influential People in The World.' This 24-year-old Hispanic actress plays the title role in the popular TV show 'Ugly Betty' and won the heart of America, and of the world.

1. Which can NOT be inferred as a factor related to the growth in Spanish? Choose two.

    ① Economic growth in Latin America
    ② Growing influence of Catholics on America
    ③ Increase in educated people using Spanish
    ④ Influence of religion on Spanish people
    ⑤ Strengthened cooperation between Latin countries

2. What do underlined parts (a) and (b) refer to?

    (a) _____   (b) _____

Speed Reading

3. What is the appropriate verb form for the blank ⓐ?

    _____

| Words | Read the following definitions and translate them into Korean. |

• **influential**: having a lot of influence over people or events _____
• **prominence**: being well known and important _____
• **immigrate**: to come to live or work in a particular country _____
• **resurgence**: reappearance, renaissance _____
• **consolidate**: to strengthen something so that it becomes more effective and secure _____
• **commerce**: the activities and procedures involved in buying and selling things _____
• **contraception**: methods of preventing pregnancy _____
• **abortion**: ending a pregnancy _____

Read the following and answer the questions.

Many Americans are concerned with the rising inmate population in the prison system. Surprisingly, the inmate population has risen by almost 80 percent over the last decade. In addition, over 50 percent of convicts will find themselves back in prison for repeat offences within 3 years of their release. The reason for this is the fact that when they get out of jail they haven't gained the proper skills to get a job, so they resort back to crime. How can we help them return to society successfully?

(A) Statistics in New York show that inmates who attend vocational training or college classes are more likely to stay out of jail once they leave. With less than 10 percent of former prisoners returning to jail, education seems to be the answer to the rising inmate problem.

(B) Researchers argue that those who get out of prison can't stay out. They harshly blame the prison system for not doing enough to rehabilitate convicts during their sentence. The prison system needs to help educate them so that they can stay out of jail after their release. Researchers stress the advantages of ⓐ hitting the books while in prison. But is a proper education really possible for inmates?

(C) In the US, education within the prison system has long been dismissed as ineffective. During the 1990s, the prison education system was severely neglected and the government made convicted criminals ineligible for the tuition aid program aimed at the poor. The government also cut the flow of money to prison education systems.

| Words | Read the following definitions and translate them into Korean. |

- **inmate:** a person who is in prison _____
- **convict:** someone who proved guilty of an offence or crime _____
- **release:** being set free from prison _____
- **vocational:** undergoing training in a special skill or trade _____
- **rehabilitate:** to reestablish the good reputation of a person _____
- **dismiss:** to discard or reject _____
- **ineffective:** useless or not working properly _____

1. What is the right order of the passage?

_____

2. Which can be inferred from the passage?

① The prison system in New York is favorable to inmates.
② Prison education may benefit prisoners, but not citizens.
③ In the U.S. criminals can apply for tuition aid programs as long as they want to study.
④ Prison education has nothing to do with the increase of the inmate population.
⑤ Inmates who receive a prison education have a better chance to stay out of jail.

3. What does the underlined part ⓐ imply?

① throwing books away
② studying hard
③ lending books
④ giving up studying
⑤ having vocational training

TIP

Guilty, But Not Going To Prison

✦ Community service is a kind of punishment for people who have violated the law. Instead of the usual imprisonment, community service gives perpetrators a chance to give something back to society. So what do they do exactly? Here are a few examples: cleaning up a park, helping senior citizens, or even lending a helping hand to farmers.

Read the following and answer the questions.

Imagine a school where the children's clothes and shoes are covered in mud. They are giggling and clutching branches and leaves in their hands. Can you guess the location of this classroom? It is outdoors. These kids are learning in the biggest classroom, through playing with nature. It's called forest kindergarten.

Forest kindergartens first appeared in Denmark in the 1950s. Mrs. Ella Plateau in Copenhagen began taking her friends' children, along with her own, into the woods every day.

Spending time in the woods became a daily routine for these children, and the parents found that playing in the forest was beneficial. But how can forest kindergartens help children's educational development?

Because of the wall free space, children are not confined or limited in their learning. They learn through their senses and observations, increasing their curiosity and creativity. The teachers in the forest kindergartens let the children play by themselves, uninterrupted. At forest kindergartens, things naturally found in the woods can provide the perfect educational tools. Children learn how to
(a) _____.

For example, rocks and acorns can be used to teach them how to add and subtract. Mud and leaves are good art material for making their own mud toy cars or leaf huts. Weather conditions such as rain or snow aren't a deterrent. The children can make their own Eskimo igloos or race leaf boats in large puddles.

The teachers don't have to insist on cooperation or community spirit. Sometimes children just need to move a very heavy fallen tree together to learn how to

cooperate. They may come across dead animals or trees from which they can learn about life and death.

As more and more people support the idea of educating in the forest, forest kindergartens are gaining popularity. There are about 300 forest kindergartens in Germany today, a number which is certain to grow as other countries catch on to this new teaching technique.

| Words | Read the following and find the words in the passage. |

- to laugh playfully: _____
- to hold something tightly: _____
- having good or helpful qualities: _____
- to prevent someone or something to go out: _____
- continuous and having no breaks: _____

1. Which is the most appropriate expression for the blank (a)?

   ① make full use of nature
   ② cooperate with each other
   ③ study math by themselves
   ④ survive in extreme conditions
   ⑤ develop their potential

2. Which best describes the kindergarten above? Choose two.

   ① Well-organized curriculum
   ② Strict regulations
   ③ Little intervention
   ④ Creative learning program
   ⑤ Up-to-dated educational facilities

3. Complete the summary by filling in the blanks with the given expressions.

   | independently | concept | outdoor | creativity | social |

   Forest kindergartens are gaining popularity as a method of early
   childhood education. These _____ schools base their
   teaching on the _____ that nature is the best teacher. Using
   things found in the forest, children can use their _____ to
   learn _____, as well as build _____ skills.
   The best part is, the children don't even know they are attending class.
   From their point of view they are just having fun!

A. Fill in the blanks with the appropriate expressions.

decade	conform	stimulate	resurgence	commerce

1. Sam does not _____ to the stereotype of being a teacher.

2. An inspiring teacher can _____ students to succeed.

3. A _____ means a period of ten years.

4. There has been a _____ of interest in politics over the last five years.

5. The department of _____ is in charge of international trade.

B. Connect each expression in column A with the matching expression in column B.

A	B
1. drastic •	• a person in prison
2. positive •	• an illness
3. inmate •	• extreme
4. disorder •	• constructive

C. Fill in the blanks with the appropriate expressions.

1. It was hard for Christians to believe _____ Darwinism.

2. Susan always wants to make use _____ the new words she learns
   in the kindergarten.

3. Paul insists _____ buying a new car for the whole family to use.

4. When you have a snack, try to drink water or milk instead _____ coke.

D. Fill in the blanks with the appropriate expressions. Use the given words.

1. Plato was a highly _____ philosopher but not an important politician. (influence)

2. The World Cup played a _____ role in the rise of public interest in soccer. (prominence)

3. He was considered to be an _____ as his parents came from India to live in the U.S. (immigrate)

4. A break is a short _____ from work. (interrupt)

5. Computers do not always have _____ effects on children. (benefit)

E. Choose the best word to complete each sentence.

1. The two companies _____ their assets to become a market leader.
   ① camouflaged   ② consolidated   ③ confined   ④ consumed

2. Most of my friends took _____ courses instead of going to university.
   ① vocational   ② occasional   ③ voluntary   ④ communal

3. As he has been working twelve hours a day for three years, he is suffering from _____.
   ① awkwardness   ② dread   ③ wrath   ④ fatigue

4. When the judge announces that the woman is guilty of murder, she is a _____ .
   ① defendant   ② counsel   ③ convict   ④ suspect

Collocation with make/ do/ have/ take

When you know the collocation,

- You can understand the meaning of the sentences that include the expressions.
- You can speed up your reading.

Collocation with make/ do/ have/ take

- **With 'make':**

make an attempt	make an application	make a conclusion
make a change	make a statement	make a speech
make an excuse	make a contribution	make progress
make a profit	make a vow	make a decision
make a claim	make a plan	make an appointment
make an arrangement	make a request	make a suggestion

- **With 'do':**

do research	do an experiment	do business
do exercise	do damage	do a good job
do a project	do(serve) time	

- **With 'have':**

have a conversation	have a good memory	have a try
have a discussion	have a fight	have an operation
have a look		

- **With 'take':**

take action	take an examination	take medicine
take a chance	take an opportunity	take advice
take counsel	take a class	

Mini Test

Which verbs best fit the blanks?

1. If you are looking for a chance to work and play at the same time, _____ this great opportunity to combine teaching English with exploring a beautiful country, Korea.

   ① make   ② do   ③ take   ④ have

2. Want to know how to _____ an application? There are two options available to you. You can use either a Full Plans or Quick Application.

   ① make   ② do   ③ take   ④ have

3. He has a constant problem with his eyes, so his eye doctor finally advised him to _____ an operation. His doctor gave him information on the most appropriate operation.

   ① make   ② do   ③ take   ④ have

4. Students should think carefully about how the results will be measured or quantified before they actually _____ an experiment.

   ① let   ② do   ③ take   ④ put

5. It is recently reported that researchers have _____ progress against an uncommon, fatal lung disease attacking pregnant women.

   ① made   ② done   ③ taken   ④ had

To fight for an idea when you have no clear idea about yourself is one of the most dangerous things you can do.
- Susanna Tamaro

Unit 2

Social Issues

Read the following and answer the questions.

Do you remember making home videos and watching them year after year at family gatherings? Every holiday, home videos make family members stars for the day. Today, however, a home video clip actually can make you an international star! With the help of 21st century mediums such as YouTube, people can share their talents worldwide.

In 2006, Esmee Denters, a 17-year-old girl from the Netherlands who was studying to become a social worker, posted a home video of herself singing pop songs on YouTube. Using her sister's webcam, Denters revealed her hidden dream of becoming a singer. This ordinary girl never expected that her dream would come true by showing her video to strangers around the world.

However, her soulful voice was quickly noticed by millions of people, and helped her land a record deal with a major record label. The new trend of sharing video clips actually gave her a chance to get noticed by millions of people, making her a global star.

Thousands of clips are posted on YouTube and other UCC sites every day. Many are from people hoping to be the next Denters, but only a few will be noticed. Of course, talent is required to impress the millions of viewers. However, if you never stop trying your best to achieve your goals, the technology of the new century can give you a second chance to finally make your dreams come true.

Words

Read the following definitions and translate them into Korean.

- **post:** to put something on an online website _____
- **hidden:** not visible, suppressed _____
- **ordinary:** everyday, not unusual _____
- **soulful:** expressing with deep emotion _____
- **impress:** to get positive feelings _____
- **achieve:** to attain, accomplish _____

1. **Which can be inferred from the passage?**

① YouTube is the most popular website around the world.

② High technology has enabled people to achieve their dreams.

③ YouTube can make every person who posts a clip famous.

④ On YouTube, technology matters more than talent.

⑤ YouTube arranged for Esmee to make a deal with an entertainment company.

Speed Reading

2. **Where should you pause during reading? Choose two.**

Esmee Denters, a 17 year ① old girl from the Netherlands who was studying to become a social worker, posted a home ② video of her singing pop songs on YouTube. Using ③ her sister's webcam, ④ she revealed her hidden dream ⑤ of becoming a singer.

3. **Write T if the statement is true. Write F if it is false.**

① Esmee became famous only in the Netherlands. _____

② Esmee's video clip was shared by millions of people online. _____

③ Modern technology allowed Esmee to show off her hidden talent. _____

TIP

A Good Craftsman Never Blames His Tools

✦ Many people think you need a big, expensive movie camera to make a good film. Is this assumption true? Many agree that what matters most is not how much you spend, but the story you tell. Recently, a 17-year-old girl made a short clip about breaking up with her boyfriend. More than 210,000 people watched it on YouTube. Some of them even bought the same camera she used to make her video on Amazon. The price was only around $100.

Read the following and answer the questions.

When people saw a white banner with nothing but "Sunyoung, I love you," written on it, they wondered what on earth it meant. Could it be a love confession from a boy who fell head over heels in love with a girl? No! Surprisingly, that banner was an advertisement.

This kind of advertisement is called a 'Teaser Advertisement.' 'Teaser' means someone who makes fun of people, often in a slightly cruel way. A 'teaser advertisement' is an advertisement that doesn't fully disclose all the information about the product being promoted. Unlike a regular advertisement, a teaser advertisement reveals just a little piece of the puzzle, which makes people more curious about the product. After a teaser advertisement, the full advertisement with the real product is revealed to satisfy people's curiosity.

For example, a famous, handsome actor appears in an advertisement, saying "Jungwon, will you marry me?," making people wonder: Who is Jungwon? Who does this handsome actor want to marry? Then a follow-up advertisement comes on, informing us that Jungwon is actually a part of a brand name, 'Chungjungwon.' Then people realize that the actor is actually promoting the brand, not saying he wants to propose. Like peeling an onion, teaser advertisements reveal product information little by little, making people more curious. As a result, people pay more attention to the advertisement and the product it is promoting.

But teaser advertisements are not always effective. Sometimes the advertisement itself receives more attention than the product or brand being advertised. People only remember (a) _____ , not (b) _____ that the advertisement initially intended to promote.

Words   Read the following definitions and translate them into Korean.

• **banner:** a long strip of cloth with something written on it _____
• **confession:** publicly telling people what you believe or feel _____
• **disclose:** to tell people about new or secret information _____
• **promote:** to try to increase the sales or popularity of a product _____
• **peel:** to remove the skin of fruit or vegetables _____
• **content:** the subject of a book/speech/TV program, the story or the idea it expresses _____
• **initially:** at first, in the beginning stages _____

1. Which is the most appropriate for blanks (a) and (b)?

(a)	(b)
① the content of the advertisement	the product or brand
② the content of the advertisement	the handsome actor
③ the brand	the handsome actor
④ the brand	the product or brand
⑤ the product	the content of the advertisement

2. Which can be inferred from the passage?

① Most advertisers use teaser advertisements.
② Teaser advertisements show all the information about the product right away.
③ Teaser advertisements consist of a pre-advertisement and the full advertisement.
④ The actual objective of teaser advertisements is to stimulate people's curiosity about the product.
⑤ Teaser advertisements are not an effective tool to promote a product.

Speed Reading

3. Where should you pause during reading? Choose two.

Like peeling an onion, teaser ① advertisements reveal product ② information little by little, ③ making people more ④ curious about the product ⑤ being advertised.

TIP

"I'm your father."

+ Have you seen the advertisement in which a shrimp says to a shrimp-flavored snack: "I'm your father."? If you've ever watched the film Star Wars, you'll recognize this scene immediately. Actually, it is a very serious moment in the original film, but, with a little twist, it becomes hilarious in the commercial. A humorous imitation of an actual event is called a parody.

Read the following and answer the questions.

What would you say if you saw a four-year-old child chained to a weaving loom? You'd probably think it was a joke and look around for a hidden camera. However, in many countries around the world this cruel image is reality. Child labor has always been a controversial and secret topic. While most people agree that the working age should be around 14 or 15 years old, in many places children as young as four are forced to do rigorous manual labor. But how is this possible?

In some cases families are so poor that all members must earn wages in order to survive, (a) _____ their age or ability. In other more extreme cases, children are kidnapped and forced to work against their will, without proper breaks, sustenance or medical care. In Egypt, for example, the small hands of children are perfect for removing bugs and other imperfections from the country's main resource, cotton. In India, children dip their hands into boiling water and inhale toxic fumes as they make thread to weave beautiful fabric.

It is not surprising that many of these child labor rings are found in poor countries, such as India or China. What is surprising is that they are also found in wealthy countries like the United States. You may also be surprised to learn that the products of child labor, such as textiles or clothing, are exported worldwide. So next time you buy new sheets, or a pair of shoes, do your best to be aware of the conditions under which they were made.

Words
Read the following definitions and translate them into Korean.

- **controversial:** causing intense public disagreement _____
- **rigorous:** intense, thorough and strict _____
- **sustenance:** the food and drink that people, animals and plants need to survive _____
- **imperfection:** flaw, small defect _____
- **inhale:** to breathe in _____
- **toxic:** poisonous _____
- **weave:** to interlace something to form a fabric or material _____
- **export:** to send or transport something, especially for trade or sale _____

1. **Which best describes the author's opinion?**

① The author thinks child laborers should ask for a raise.
② The author suggests that consumers be more aware of child labor.
③ The author believes that Egyptians are good at training children.
④ The author suggests child labor be approved as long as it is done to make a living.
⑤ The author insists that child labor is mostly found in rich countries.

2. **Which is the most appropriate expression for the blank (a)?**

① regarding
② in spite of
③ based on
④ regardless of
⑤ owing to

3. **What kinds of products are taken as examples of the products made using child labor in the passage?**

_____

 TIP

Pay the Right Price

+ Fair Trade is a social movement focusing on the ethical consumption by paying better prices and improving working conditions for farmers and workers in the developing world. It is also a way of environmentally-friendly production system. If you want to support Fair Trade, the easiest way is to buy fair trade products.

Read the following and answer the questions.

How do you picture the cities of the future? Do fast-paced, high-density urban environments such as Hong Kong or Tokyo come to mind? Or maybe you imagine entire cities enclosed in one mega-structure. Believe it or not, the cities of the future may be the exact opposite. A movement called Slow Cities is taking the world by storm and gaining increased popularity. But what exactly is a Slow City?

The city of Greve in Chianti, a picturesque town in Tuscany, Italy, was the first of the slow cities. Residents of Greve in Chianti live off of wine and olive oil production and export, and boast a healthy economy. The people of Greve in Chianti are in equally good health, eating only local produce grown in the lush countryside of their backyards. Pollution is not evident, as cars are discouraged ⓐ _____ entering the city center, and only sustainable energy is used.

Slow cities such as Greve in Chianti focus on quality of life and encourage people to lead a relaxed lifestyle. The goal is to simplify life, giving inhabitants the opportunity to (a) _____.
In slow cities, the use of local produce and products are encouraged. Slow cities also cut down ⓑ _____ noise pollution and crowds, and promote creativity and individualism within the community.

Being granted the title of Slow City is not easy. Cities must have less than 50,000 residents and be checked routinely to make sure they are following the required environmental and urban policies. If you ever find yourself craving a relaxed way of life, why not consider living in a Slow City?

Words   Read the following definitions and translate them into Korean.

• **density:** compactness, closely set or crowded condition _____
• **urban:** belonging to or relating to a city _____
• **enclose:** to surround completely _____
• **evident:** obvious, easily noticeable _____
• **discourage:** to deter certain behavior _____
• **sustainable:** being able to be maintained _____
• **inhabitant:** someone or something that lives somewhere _____

1. **Which of the following can be said as a feature of Slow Cities?**

   ① Cities encouraging the export of their products
   ② Cities with mega-structure buildings
   ③ Cities encouraging the use of imported produce
   ④ Cities encouraging the use of renewable energy
   ⑤ Cities which look similar to Tokyo

2. **Which is the most appropriate expression for the blank (a)?**

   ① lead a fast-paced life
   ② keep up with the times
   ③ live a traditional and eco-friendly existence
   ④ give up social interaction with others
   ⑤ try to produce better yields

3. **What are the appropriate prepositions for blanks ⓐ and ⓑ?**

   ⓐ _____   ⓑ _____

TIP

Tomorrow Will Be Better... Or Not?

+ In Science Fiction (SF) films and novels, the world of the future is sometimes described as a gloomy and dark place where life is extremely hard. Whether it be a cruel dictatorship where people's rights are limited, a situation where only a few people survive a major epidemic, or a society where technology has advanced but humanity had regressed, SF can paint a grim picture. This kind of society is called a dystopia, the opposite of utopia.

Read the following and answer the questions.

People usually assume that the news represents the world accurately. People think what is shown in the news is real, believable, and unbiased. But does the news really show the world as it is? For a long time, the objectivity of the news has been a critical issue in journalism as there are so many factors that can affect its objectivity. Journalists say there are 3 major reasons why it is difficult for the news to be absolutely objective.

The most important reason is the limitation of time and space. For example, the limited space of a newspaper forces editors (a) <u>to decide / deciding</u> which stories will appear and which will be overlooked. The 'judgment' of the editor is, in itself, a form of bias. It is difficult to expect any human being to be absolutely fair and objective, therefore, the editor's values influence the process of news making. Deadlines pose another limitation on the kind of stories covered in the newspaper. Events which occur after the deadline are hard to include in today's paper.

The second factor is economical reasons. News companies need financial support to produce the news. Although readers pay for the news, a large portion of financial support comes from advertisers. In addition to (b) <u>place/ placing</u> advertisements, advertisers sometimes want to influence the way a news story is reported, especially when the news story involves the advertiser.

The last reason comes from the political power of the government. Even though this is not such a serious issue nowadays, in some developing countries governments still do their best to control news media.

But even if objectivity is an ideal goal for journalists and editors (c) <u>to fulfill/ to be fulfilled</u>, it is also true that people ultimately expect fair and objective news. This is why objective reporting has to become the top priority of journalists.

1. Which of the following best describes the writer's opinion?
   Choose two.

   ① Government supports news companies for fair competition.
   ② Sometimes something in the news can be biased.
   ③ Many news companies tend to place only popular articles.
   ④ Advertisers should not affect journalists too much.
   ⑤ A journalist's goal is to report objective news.

2. What is the most appropriate for each underlined part? Choose
   the correct one.

   (a) _____   (b) _____   (c) _____

3. Complete the summary by filling in the blanks with the given
   expressions.

   | fair | constraint | barrier | independent | destination |

   Due to various reasons, it is often difficult to produce completely
   _____ and objective news. Time _____ is
   the biggest _____ for journalists, along with limited
   space. Economic and political power also makes it hard for the media to
   become fully _____. Even so, objective reporting must
   become the final _____ for news reporters.

   | **Words** | Read the following definitions and find the words in the passage. |

   - to believe something to be true, sometimes wrongly: _____
   - fair and not likely to support one particular person or group: _____
   - an important subject people are discussing: _____
   - a situation that allows only some actions, making others impossible: _____
   - finally, after a long and complicated series of events: _____
   - based on facts rather than on one's personal feelings: _____

A. Fill in the blanks with the appropriate expressions.

| imperfection | density | medium | limitation | confession |

1. The Internet is used as a _____ to express ourselves.

2. After hours and hours of investigation, the suspect finally made a full

   _____ .

3. We all make mistakes, thus, need to love _____ to improve
   our relationship.

4. Seoul has the highest population _____.

5. Her accomplishment was said to exceed the _____s of human ability.

B. Connect each expression in column A with the matching expression in column B.

A	B
1. ordinary •	• easygoing
2. effective •	• average
3. rigorous •	• efficient
4. relaxed •	• strict
5. unbiased •	• fair

C. Fill in the blanks with the appropriate expressions.

1. His talent finally got noticed _____ professional soccer scouts.

2. Now many international companies pay more attention _____ the benefits
   for staff.

3. I am fully aware _____ the risk I might encounter if I go ahead with this plan.

4. The professor focused _____ how scientific technology made recent advancements.

5. You can pay _____ your purchases here by cash, if you're willing to.

D. Fill in the blanks with the appropriate expressions. Use the given words.

1. In this section, _____ files and systems may not be presented properly. (hide)

2. The government has heightened activities regulating exaggerated _____. (advertise)

3. It is totally _____ that he, at the age of 90, still works out at a gym everyday. (surprise)

4. Our attempts to make _____ communities will improve everyone's quality of life. (sustain)

E. Choose the best word to complete each sentence.

1. Diana Krall, one of the bestselling jazz vocalists, is well known for her _____ voice.
   ① notorious   ② large   ③ infamous   ④ soulful

2. In order to _____ foreign investment, we should reform our business regulations.
   ① divide   ② promote   ③ brighten   ④ supply

3. In the country, five million _____ rely on hunting and fishing.
   ① habitation   ② inhabitation   ③ inhabitants   ④ habitat

4. A lot of companies _____ that online marketing is an effective way to attract new customers.
   ① prefer   ② activate   ③ assume   ④ reach

Text Chunking

What is 'Chunk'?

A segment of words in a sentence which is grouped together to given an even flow when reading.

When you know the Text Chunking,

- You can understand the structure of long sentences better.
- You can comprehend the meaning of the sentences faster.
- You can accelerate your reading speed.

Text Chunking involves breaking down sentences into non-overlapping units on the basis of 'meaning.' Here are a few ways of chunking:

A. Subject / Predicates

Enjoying the mild breeze, many people / are swimming in the pool.

B. Coordinate clauses (independent clauses)

It / breezed all day / and many people / had a good time at the pool.

C. Subordinate clauses (dependent clauses)

1. Noun clauses
   - Many people / are talking about how they can get a great tan.
2. Adjective clauses
   - Many people / who are swimming in the pool / wear stripped swim suits.
3. Adverb clauses
   - Many people / were swimming / when I got to the pool.

D. Phrases

1. Prepositional phrases
   - Many people / are swimming / and getting a tan at the pool.
2. Participial phrases
   - Swimming and getting a tan, many people / have a good relaxing time.

Mini Test

Put a slash mark (/) between the subjects and the predicates.

1. Solar energy used at the Olympic site   will lower operation costs.

2. After thirteen hours of work, leisure time   should be spent mostly in reading.

3. An employee, who is in the habit of smoking cigars,   will surely give his employer reason to be suspicious of his honesty and integrity.

Underline the dependent clause in the sentence.

4. The U.S. / should keep in mind / that being the world's only superpower is associated with political and moral responsibilities.

5. I was walking through the mall the other day / when I witnessed an interesting example of parenting.

Underline the two independent clauses.

6. Graph drawing is a type of data visualization, / but it is different from other types of visualization in terms of its many aspects.

Experience is a hard teacher because she gives the test first, the lesson afterwards.
- Vernon Saunders Law

Unit 3

Places & Politics

Read the following and answer the questions.

Are you tired (a) _____ taking the same old vacation? Do you want to challenge yourself in a remote location? If so, start packing! We have the perfect vacation for you! At the Bonamanzi Game Park in South Africa you will sleep in a tree house for 5 nights and share your yard with wart hogs, elephants and lions. You will return home with a new perspective on life, in addition to incredible memories and photos.

Be prepared: these houses do have some amenities, but they are very rustic. You'll have to boil your own water and cook your own food. The houses are isolated, so you will get a chance to really experience nature as you fall asleep to the sounds (a) _____ animals prowling and locals chanting. Leave your dress shoes at home. Your best asset here is a comfortable pair of sandals, cargo pants and a tank top. Don't forget sunscreen and mosquito repellent!

Your day will begin bright and early at 5 a.m. During your stay you will spend your mornings (b) _____ guided wildlife safaris. Afternoons and evenings will be spent exploring local sights such as the hippopotamus reserve at the town of St. Lucia. So next time you get the urge to go (b) _____ vacation, call us first. We promise you a trip you'll never forget!

Words   Read the following definitions and translate them into Korean.

- **perspective:** the way of thinking about something _____
- **amenity:** things provided for people's convenience _____
- **rustic:** basic or unsophisticated _____
- **isolated:** far away and difficult to reach _____
- **prowl:** to move around quietly, often when hunting _____
- **repellent:** a spray used to keep insects away _____
- **reserve:** an area of land where animals and plants are protected _____

1. Who might be most interested in the passage?

① A person who is interested in nutritious food
② A person who wants to experience high tech culture
③ A person who wants to travel in comfort
④ A person who wants to guide people on wildlife safaris
⑤ A person who wants to experience wilderness

Speed Reading

2. What are the appropriate prepositions for blanks (a) and (b)?

(a) _____   (b) _____

3. Write T if the statement is true. Write F if it is false.

① In the Bonamanzi Game Park, it is easy to see an elephant. _____

② Tourists will go on a safari on their own. _____

③ Luxury accommodation and food will be offered to tourists. _____

 TIP

One Very Cold Summer Night

✦ What are your plans this summer vacation? Have you ever dreamed of spending the summer in a "very cool" place, escaping the suffocating heat? If so, you should stay at an ice hotel. From floor to ceiling, ice hotels are made entirely from snow and ice. Even the furniture is ice! Spending a night in an ice hotel is an original and memorable experience.

Read the following and answer the questions.

Can you imagine an observatory without telescopes or other modern equipment? Probably not. But, when you think about it, people were aware of the changes in the sun, moon and stars long before the first modern telescope was built. Take the Jantar Mantar in New Delhi, India, for example. Completed in 1774, the Jantar

Mantar was one of five observatories built by Sawai Jai Singh II to make accurate and up-to-date almanacs and astronomical charts.

Instead of high-tech devices, the Jantar Mantar used large scale masonry instruments to determine the exact location of the sun, moon and other planets, and even tell time. Its centerpiece is a huge sundial, called the Samrat Yantra, or Supreme Instrument, which could tell time accurately to the second. Three other instruments were used to predict eclipses, summer and winter solstices and world time. Legend has (a) _____ this observatory even ended heated debates between Muslim and Hindu sects over the positions of the planets.

Can we still benefit from the Jantar Mantar? Unfortunately not, as its accuracy is now compromised by the many tall buildings surrounding it. Nevertheless, the structure is well preserved and still serves as a landmark and reminder of past astronomical achievements. In fact, it is so modern in design that those unfamiliar with its long history may think the observatory is a piece of modern art.

Words

Read the following definitions and translate them into Korean.

- **observatory:** a place with equipment used to observe stars and the planets _____
- **almanac:** a yearly publication containing information about the planets, moon phases, etc. _____
- **centerpiece:** the biggest and best of a number of things _____
- **eclipse:** the phenomenon during which the sun or moon is partially or completely blocked from view _____
- **solstice:** two days out of the year when the sun is farthest from the equator _____
- **compromise:** to reach an acceptable agreement _____
- **landmark:** an easily recognizable building or feature which can be used to pinpoint the location _____

1. Which can be inferred from the passage?

① The Jantar Mantar proves the importance of modern devices.
② The Jantar Mantar was built after the invention of a telescope.
③ Indians found out the location of the sun and moon in the 18th century.
④ The Samrat Yantra is a predecessor of modern telescopes.
⑤ The Jantar Mantar is the only observatory that was built by
   Sawai Jai Singh II.

Speed Reading

2. What is the most appropriate for the blank (a)?

has _____

3. Match the main idea with each paragraph.

Paragraph 1 •   • The Jantar Mantar today

Paragraph 2 •   • What Jantar Mantar is

Paragraph 3 •   • How Jantar Mantar was used

TIP

Why Monaco?

+ Monaco is a small country located in Western Europe. On the coast of the
  Mediterranean Sea, its beautiful scenery attracts many tourists. It is also famous
  for being a tax haven, therefore many of its inhabitants are wealthy foreigners.

Read the following and answer the questions.

The Alhambra is one of many buildings that have inspired artists, architects and composers from all over the world. In terms of beauty and elaborate design, only a few can rival it. Washington Irving, the 19th century American writer, praised its beauty in his Tales of the Alhambra.

The name Alhambra - meaning "the red one" - is believed to come from the color of the bricks used in its construction. It is located in the city of Granada, Spain. It is not a single building, but rather, a combination of palaces, towers, courtyards, fountains, gardens, and villas. Once you step inside, you will be enchanted by fabulous Arabic inscriptions and geometric patterns. The elaborate decorations and lace-like artistic designs on the ceilings and walls are also

_____ (more, attract, enough) the attention of the many visitors.

No wonder King Boabdil, the last king of Granada, cried when he had to hand over the Alhambra to the Catholics. Unfortunately, the Alhambra underwent various changes. As a result, it was severely damaged and some of the towers were destroyed. In spite of the damage, the Alhambra managed to survive and finally became a part of the UNESCO World Heritage List in 1984.

| Words | Read the following definitions and translate them into Korean. |

- **rival:** to compete with something _____
- **enchant:** to give a feeling of delight or pleasure _____
- **inscription:** a written thing carved into something _____
- **geometric:** of patterns or shapes made up of regular lines _____
- **undergo:** to experience something necessary or unpleasant _____
- **damage:** injury or harm to a person or thing _____

1. Which is NOT mentioned in the passage?

   ① The architecture of the Alhambra
   ② The origin of the name, "Alhambra"
   ③ Historical facts about the Alhambra
   ④ An American writer's remarks about the Alhambra
   ⑤ The name of the King who constructed the Alhambra

2. Which can NOT be inferred from the passage?

   ① The Alhambra influenced Arabic architecture.
   ② The Alhambra was built with red bricks.
   ③ The Alhambra went through many changes.
   ④ The Alhambra was a source of inspiration for many artists.
   ⑤ The Alhambra is one of the most beautiful buildings in the world.

Speed Reading

3. What is the most appropriate expression for the blank?
   Use the given words.

_____

TIP

The Most Beautiful Tomb in the World

+ The Taj Mahal is one of the most beautiful structures in the world. In the 17th century, Mughal Emperor, Shah Jahan, lost his beloved wife and ordered this white marble mausoleum to be built in her honor. The Taj Mahal is a UNESCO World Heritage Site and was cited as "the jewel of Muslim art in India."

Read the following and answer the questions.

Can you believe that a country could exist for only one day of the year? This is the case in a country named Uzupis. It is a tiny district within the borders of the Lithuanian town of Vilnius. The area lies on the edge of the Vilnia River, and is partially located in the Old Town of Vilnius. This means that, like the Vatican City within the boundaries of the city of Rome, it is technically a tiny country of only 148 acres. Vilnius, where Uzupis is located, is designated a UNESCO World Heritage Site.

Artists who live in the small area declared Uzupis an independent republic as a joke on April Fool's Day in 1997. Since then, every April Fool's Day, it is called the Uzupis Republic, and recognized as an independent country.

You even need a visa to get into the area on April 1ˢᵗ, which is universally considered to be a day (a) _____ _____ . This is thought to keep up with the sense of humor of the constitution of Uzupis, which contains some rather unusual articles.

Nowadays, Uzupis is known primarily for its artistic endeavors. Even its current President is himself a poet, musician and film director. In 2001, a statue of an angel blowing a trumpet was erected in the main square of Uzupis, which (b) _____ (intend, symbolize) the revival of artistic freedom in the district. There are over 200 ambassadors whose mission is to acquaint the world with Uzupis' artistic freedom.

Words   Read the following definitions and translate them into Korean.

- **border:** a dividing line between two areas _____
- **designate:** to choose someone to do a particular job _____
- **heritage:** traditions or qualities that have been continued over long periods of time _____
- **constitution:** a system of laws of a country _____
- **article:** a section of a formal agreement which deals with a particular point _____
- **acquaint:** to become familiar with someone or something _____

1. **Which is true according to the passage?**

　① Uzupis borders lie within the Vatican city.

　② UNESCO declared Uzupis an independent republic.

　③ Uzupis represents a revival of artistic spirit.

　④ People need a visa to gain admission to Uzupis all year round.

　⑤ Uzupis and Lithuania have fought over their territories.

2. **Which is the most appropriate expression for the blank (a)?**

　① ambassadors are praised for their art

　② many people perform practical jokes

　③ which symbolizes artistic freedom

　④ a statue of an angel was erected

　⑤ people in Uzupis rejoice their independence

Speed Reading

3. **What is the most appropriate for the blank (b)? Use the given words.**

_____

There Is No Greenwich Observatory in Greenwich

✦ Greenwich is actually a part of London. It is best known for the Royal Observatory, and as the home of the Greenwich Meridian (zero degrees longitude) and Greenwich Mean Time. Ironically, the Royal Greenwich Observatory is not located in Greenwich anymore. Due to light pollution in London, the observatory itself was moved to Herstmonceux Castle. The old observatory building is now used as a museum.

Read the following and answer the questions.

If you were asked to go on vacation to Sichuan, the epicenter of a recent earthquake, how would you feel? Along with Niagara Falls and the Forbidden City in China, unique places such as Ground Zero in New York and the site of the Oklahoma City bombing attract a lot of visitors.

These sites represent disaster, death and suffering, yet millions of tourists from all over the world flock to them every year. For most, these sorrowful locations have just as much impact as popular tourist destinations. These places overwhelm people with the strong emotions they provoke.

The expression 'Dark Tourism' is used to describe people's interest in these sites of death and suffering. Although some people are strongly against the idea of opening these sorrowful scenes to the public, it would be meaningful if used to educate witnesses and make sure that history doesn't repeat itself.

(A) Going to New Orleans gives tourists a chance to absorb the Southern American culture and lifestyle. Along with delicious soul food such as jambalaya and hush puppies, New Orleans is the site of one of the world's largest parties, Mardi Gras. Although the face of the city has changed, due to the destruction of hurricane Katrina, the spirit remains the same.

(B) Many people visit concentration camps such as Auschwitz to understand the plight of Jewish people during Hitler's reign. However, a more personal experience can be had by visiting Anne Frank's home in Amsterdam. Once behind the secret bookcase that disguised her hiding place, it's possible to experience some of the fear and secrecy of the time.

(C) After basking in the sunrise at Angkor Watt, many tourists move on to a more macabre scene: the Killing Fields. This mass graveyard is one of the most disturbing sites in Cambodia, if not in the world. Every year tourists spend a lot of money in order to witness man's inhumanity to man.

1. What is this passage mainly about?

　① World famous tourist destinations
　② Various ways to learn history
　③ The definition of Dark Tourism and some popular Dark tourism sites
　④ Why people are interested in Dark Tourism
　⑤ Changes in people's preference for travel sites

2. To what paragraph can the spirit of "Dark tourism" be applied?

　_____

3. Complete the summary by filling in the blanks with the given expressions.

take advantage	valuable	grief	tragic

Some tourists visit _____ places including Ground Zero in New York. Others blame Dark Tourism for making it popular to _____ of others' _____ . However, visiting sorrowful places can teach people _____ lessons.

Words	Read the following definitions and find the words in the passage.

• to go somewhere in large numbers: _____
• to instigate or cause something: _____
• to see something with one's own eyes: _____
• a distressing situation: _____
• to hide something from view: _____
• a place where humans are buried after death: _____

A. Fill in the blanks with the appropriate expressions.

> concentration   construction   perspective   achievement   endeavor

1. Some people have a different _____ on life.

2. We are going to assess your level of academic _____ .

3. I'd like to announce that the parking lot will be inaccessible due to _____ .

4. Our party made every _____ to bring freedom and peace in this country.

5. During the World War II, many innocent people were put into _____ camps.

B. Connect each expression in column A with the matching expression in column B.

A	B
1. incredible •	• marvelous
2. accurate •	• exact
3. fabulous •	• amazing
4. independent •	• significant
5. meaningful •	• autonomous

C. Fill in the blanks with the appropriate expressions.

1. _____ addition to art therapy, music therapy will help children in trouble.

2. There is a huge debate _____ supporters and opposers of the issue.

3. This book has lots of fruitful discussions in terms _____ globalization.

4. Andy Warhol, a famous American Artist, is best known _____ his whimsical Pop Art.

5. Click the Next button to move _____ to the next step.

D. **Fill in the blanks with the appropriate expressions. Use the given words.**

1. Thanks to insect _____ , you can play and work outdoors without
   the risk of insect bites. (repel)
2. Galileo's _____ findings were one of the most influential achievements.
   (astronomy)
3. Dr. Long has been suffering _____ from diabetes. (severe)
4. Researchers and economists have agreed that we are now _____
   in a recession. (technical)
5. Irresponsible administration may result in _____ consequences. (disaster)

E. **Choose the best word to complete each sentence.**

1. Surprisingly, many people enjoy taking trips to _____ areas.
   ① remote   ② united   ③ sparkling   ④ provincial

2. For future generations, we should _____ our cultural heritage.
   ① select   ② present   ③ spend   ④ preserve

3. He _____ a surgical operation while he was in the army.
   ① underwent   ② accused   ③ depended   ④ followed

4. The government _____ this tree as a precious natural treasure.
   ① investigated   ② appealed   ③ designated   ④ succeeded

5. His attempts to _____ the truth from people were in vain.
   ① remember   ② disguise   ③ inspect   ④ relate

Idiomatic Expressions

Why do you need to study idiomatic expressions?

- Text comprehension is proven to be deeply related to idiom comprehension.
- Idioms are what give writing a natural flow.
  ⇒ A person lacking knowledge of idiomatic expressions can misunderstand others or cause others to misunderstand.
- You cannot guess the meaning of the idiomatic expressions since the meaning is different from the individual words which form it.

Common English idiomatic expressions

- prevent (keep, stop, prohibit, hinder) A from B: make A not do something to B

  To prevent patients from trying to scam money out of insurance companies, medical institutions have to share information about suspected fraud.

- so adjective that S cannot V ⇒ too adjective to V

  In the morning they are so busy getting off to work that they cannot have time for conversation. ⇒ In the morning they are too busy getting off to work to have time for conversation.

- so adjective that S can V ⇒ enough to V

  The number of passengers aboard were so numerous that the ship could sink.
  ⇒ The number of passengers aboard were numerous enough to sink the ship.

Confusing English idiomatic expressions

1. be used to + N: The subject is accustomed to something.
   The younger generation (is used to) the two-way communication of the Internet.
   cf) be used + to-V: The subject is used in order to do something.
   One serious hold up had been the use of fertilized chicken eggs, which (are used to produce) all influenza vaccines.

2. be sure of -ing: The subject is confident that the subject will do something.
   Germany is sure of making the finals.

   be sure to -v: The speaker is confident that the subject will do something.
   Eating fast food daily is sure to lead ones to obesity.

Mini Test

Choose the most appropriate expression for each blank.

1. There are _____ thousands of deaths due to the outbreak of diseases such as cholera.

   ① at being   ② of being   ③ to be

2. Korean beef negotiation team is said to have suggested the U.S. government operate a separate Export Verification (EV) program to prevent over 30-month old animals _____ being exported to Korea.

   ① by   ② from   ③ under

3. Rose Motors Corporation, must pay $6 million to the owners for a defective brake system design that caused parts to wear _____ prematurely

   ① about   ② on   ③ out

4. Cars are marvelous inventions, but they have so many side effects. Cars produce _____ much pollution that they can affect our health.

   ① very   ② so   ③ too

Put the words in the brackets in the correct order.

5. They were disappointed because they did not have (votes / to / enough / pass) the meat inspection.

   _____

The main goal of golf is to learn to accept what can't be altered and keep on doing one's own resolute best.
- Bobby Jones

Unit 4

Sports & Economy

Read the following and answer the questions.

Would you believe a 17-year-old girl became a CEO of a million-dollar company in three years with only eight dollars? Not so long ago, Ashley Qualls lived in a one-bedroom apartment with her mom and sister. But, by using her computer and business sense, she made a better life for all of them.

Unlike other typical high school students, Ashley is the head of whateverlife.com, a website she started when she was just 14, with eight dollars borrowed from her mother. Now the website grosses more than $1 million a year, providing Ashley and her working class family with a sense of security they had never really known.

Ashley became interested in graphic design just as the online social networking craze began to catch on. When she saw her friends personalizing their MySpace pages, she began creating and giving away background designs through her website. The designs are creative, colorful, and whimsical. "Teenage girls love my designs," Ashley says, scrolling through some of her site's 3,000 designs, more than a third of which she made herself.

When the first check arrived, her mother was doubtful, wondering if her daughter could really make money off a website. But Ashley was right. The checks kept coming and the business kept growing — to the point where she could afford to buy a brand new four-bedroom house. Thanks to $8 and creative determination, Ashley proved that you don't have to be old to be rich.

| Words | Read the following definitions and translate them into Korean. |

- **typical**: normal, usual _____
- **gross**: to earn a particular amount of money before deductions _____
- **security**: feeling of safety _____
- **craze**: trend that is popular with people _____
- **personalize**: to make something reflect one's own personality _____
- **whimsical**: describing an idea or concept which is unusual or playful _____
- **determination**: a drive to accomplish a goal _____

1. **Which best describes Ashley's personality?**

① rigid and reserved
② aggressive and reserved
③ determined and ambitious
④ dependent and flexible
⑤ practical and passive

2. **What is the closest in meaning to "start booming" in the above passage? Write in two words.**

_____

3. **Write T if the statement is true. Write F if it is false.**

① Ashley was born into a wealthy family. _____

② Designing web pages inspired Ashley to run a business. _____

③ Ashley made all of the site's designs by herself. _____

 TIP

From Garage Geek to Billionaire

✦ In 2005, three former PayPal employees created a website that allowed users to upload, view, and share video clips. Their early office was a makeshift one, run out of a garage. They had also run up a sizable credit card debt launching the site. However, the site grew remarkably in a very short time. On October 16, 2006, their website, YouTube, was sold to Google for a whopping $1.65 billion.

Read the following and answer the questions.

Who hasn't dreamt of getting rich overnight? Many people try to make a lot of money quickly by investing in stocks. However, the stock market can be rewarding but risky. Success is not guaranteed, and some investors even lose money! If you want to get involved in stock trading, there are some important guidelines to follow.

The first rule of the stock market is "Don't invest money you can't afford to lose." Most advisors also suggest investing in companies or products you are already familiar with. And remember the saying: _____ Rather than investing all your cash in one stock, let a stockbroker help you create a balanced portfolio with a variety of long-term, short-term and cyclical stocks.

If you're determined to invest on your own you can always practice first. Many websites offer opportunities for individuals to "invest" in stocks online using pretend money. These sites allow potential investors to learn about fundamentals — such as earnings, growth, the value of a stock, and dividend ratios — risk free. By learning the basics beforehand, you will be more likely to make a much higher profit in the future.

| Words | Read the following definitions and translate them into Korean. |

- **invest:** to buy shares in a company _____
- **stock:** shares in a company _____
- **rewarding:** satisfying _____
- **portfolio:** all investments and stocks held by a person _____
- **cyclical:** happening again and again in the same order _____
- **dividend:** the percentage of a company's earnings which is paid to its shareholders _____

1. **Which is the appropriate saying for the blank?**

① Don't put all your eggs in one basket.
② Lost time is never found.
③ A small leak can sink a ship.
④ Fish and guests stink after three days.
⑤ Don't count your chickens before they've hatched.

2. **Which does the writer suggest that investors do?**

① Invest money in banks rather than stocks.
② Try to find an expert on online stock trading.
③ Invest more money in stocks online.
④ Don't be afraid of making mistakes.
⑤ Be aware of basic rules first.

3. **Match the main idea with each paragraph.**

Paragraph 1 •   • Reducing the risk of losing money
                          when investing in stocks

Paragraph 2 •   • A warning to potential investors to
                          follow guidelines

Paragraph 3 •   • Practice investing online before using
                          real money

TIP

A $4 Million Seat

+ The New York Stock Exchange (NYSE) is the largest stock exchange in the world. The combined capital of all New York Stock Exchange listed companies is $25 trillion. In 2005, the cost of a membership was $4 million!

Read the following and answer the questions.

If you had a chance to buy a Van Gogh or a Picasso for only $8.00, would you? Every year many people go to the Art Village in Defen, China, to take advantage of deals just like this. Anyone, from tourists to big-box companies such as Wal-Mart, is able to buy cheap art from the masters. But there is a catch. These mass-produced paintings are all fakes. But how did this village get its start?

The founding father of this lucrative village was Huang Jiang, who arrived at the once barren town as an entrepreneur with a goal to mass-produce art. He achieved his goal with great success. But now, with 8,000 to 10,000 artists hard at work, the competition is stiff and not as (a) <u>financially rewarding</u> as it once was. However, (b) <u>this</u> doesn't hinder the village from producing around 5 million knock-off paintings per year.

Of course, there is some controversy surrounding the ethics of mass-reproducing original pieces of art. If the masters could witness their creations being reproduced on an assembly line, they'd probably turn over in their graves. Luckily (c) <u>they</u> are no longer around to witness what China considers a proud example of its cultural industry. Despite the fraudulent undertones, the paintings are sold as imitations only. The art village is a good example of the saying "imitation is the sincerest form of flattery."

| Words | Read the following definitions and translate them into Korean. |

- **catch:** a hidden problem or difficulty _____
- **lucrative:** making money or a profit _____
- **mass-produce:** to make many of the same thing at once _____
- **stiff competition:** intense rivalry between talented competitors _____
- **knock-off:** a fake but similar-looking version of the original _____
- **fraudulent:** deceitful _____
- **undertone:** an underlying quality, not immediately obvious _____
- **flattery:** paying a compliment _____

1. **Which is the appropriate expression for the blank below?**

> In spite of controversy, people visit Defen _____ .

① to purchase masters' art at lower prices
② to learn how to create cheap art pieces
③ to enjoy original pieces of art
④ to mass-produce more fake paintings
⑤ to witness art pieces created on an assembly line

2. **What is the closet in meaning to the underlined part (a)?**
   Find the word in the passage.

   _____

Speed Reading

3. **What do underlined parts (b) and (c) refer to? Find the expressions in the passage?**

   (b) the fact that _____

   _____

   (c) _____

TIP

Life's Ironies

+ Lee Joong-sup (1916-1956) is one of Korea's most well-known modernist artists. During his lifetime, he suffered from poverty. Some of his most famous works were drawn on cigarette pack papers. Ironically, today his paintings cost a fortune and forgeries are abundant.

Read the following and answer the questions.

Running and music have been associated for a long time. Experts agree that having your favorite tunes playing while you workout can really get you training hard. ⓐ One of the most popular names in shoes and ⓑ one of the most popular names in digital entertainment have teamed up to give you the ultimate workout experience. Nike and Apple Computers have collaborated to create the newest technological advancement that will have runners pounding the pavement once again.

(A) ⓒ This allows you to see your runs, set goals, and challenge friends. Apple and Nike have created an online community where runners can compare their personal statistics. You can even compete with friends or strangers around the world by challenging them to a virtual run anytime and anywhere.

(B) Furthermore, it records several different aspects of your run, such as distance, time, pace, and calories burnt. You can set your run to target any of these different categories. Your iPod can store and display 1000 workout sessions, so you can view your workout information whenever you want. Once your workout is done, your workout data is sent to Apple's iTunes program and nikeplus.com.

(C) This new innovation uses the Apple iPod, a pair of compatible Nike+ shoes, and the new Nike+ iPod Sport Kit. The Sport Kit is inserted into the running shoes and then shares information about your workout with your iPod. Your iPod then becomes your own personal trainer and gives you workout-based voice progress reports.

(D) Don't you agree that running just became a lot more fun? If you need to get pumped up for an especially strenuous workout, you can program your "power song" into your iPod. It will give you extra inspiration when you need it the most.

| Words | Read the following definitions and translate them into Korean. |

- **associate:** to connect or bring into relation, as a thought, feeling or memory _____
- **collaborate:** to work together with two or more partners, usually on a project _____
- **virtual:** of an electronic representation of something real _____
- **compatible:** capable of being used with equipment in a system _____
- **strenuous:** difficult or tiring _____
- **inspiration:** an exciting thought _____

1. Which is the correct order of the passage?

① (A) - (B) - (C) - (D)
② (A) - (C) - (B) - (D)
③ (B) - (C) - (A) - (D)
④ (C) - (A) - (B) - (D)
⑤ (C) - (B) - (A) - (D)

2. What do underlined parts Ⓜ and Ⓟ respectively refer to?

Ⓜ _____ Ⓟ _____

Speed Reading

3. What does the underlined part ⓖ refer to? Write the content using the correct expression in the passage.

The fact that _____

_____ .

Run, Rain or Shine

+ Many people go jogging to stay healthy and fit. But going out running is not always easy; what if it rains or snows? Or perhaps there isn't a suitable place to run in your neighborhood. In these cases, a treadmill can be a good alternative. Rain or shine, you can run anytime you want. But don't forget, you'll still need a good pair of running shoes even if you are running on the treadmill!

Read the following and answer the questions.

The Super Bowl is a must-see television event for millions of viewers in North America. During the final game, the streets are empty, long-distance calls drop by 50% and fewer weddings take place. Along with the popularity of the super bowl, advertisers are willing to pay $2.7 million dollars for 30 seconds of airtime for their commercials. Not only do viewers tune in to watch the big game, they also want to watch to be among the first to see the debut of the fantastic commercials aired during the game. What do you think? Does this sound reasonable?

(A) Writer A: In reality, people watching the game think most of the commercials are hilarious and they become huge fans of them. For instance, Budweiser beer commercials featuring talking frogs caught people's attention immediately. This illustrates clearly why advertisers value the airtime so highly. Some people still doubt if the astronomical cost of airtime for the commercials is money well-spent. However, advertisers feel that this showcase event gives them a huge bang for their buck.

(B) Writer B: A recent survey revealed that two out of every five Super Bowl viewers actually tune in for the commercials. For many fans, the high-budget ads are part of the <u>draw</u>. With the cost of Super Bowl advertising getting higher and higher every year, only the biggest name-brands are willing to shell out the cash necessary for a 30-second spot. These entertaining ads are a source of joy and humor throughout the year, but ultimately it's the consumer who pays the cost of the advertising. Therefore, viewers must be careful not to gamble their money away on products that are advertised during this big event.

| Words | Read the following definitions and find the words in the passage. |

• an advertisement played on television: _____
• the first public appearance: _____
• very funny: _____
• the time during which a television show or advertisement is viewed by people: _____
• getting good value for money: _____
• finally, eventually after a long and complicated series of events: _____

1. **Which best describes the writer A's opinion?**

① Super Bowl ads are too expensive.
② Fun ads are becoming more competitive in the market.
③ Advertisers should come up with more economical ads.
④ The higher the viewers' interest, the better the ads become.
⑤ Airtime during the Super Bowl is valuable to both advertisers and viewers.

2. **Which is the closest in meaning to the underlined word, 'draw' in (B)?**

① to breathe deeply once
② an attention grabbing attraction
③ to use a pencil and produce a picture
④ pulling something our of a container
⑤ a competition where people pay money for named tickets

3. **Complete the summary by filling in the blanks with the given expressions.**

| competition | value | commercials | advertisers | airtime |

Super Bowl _____ are the most watched advertisements in the world. The _____ has pushed the price of _____ higher and higher. Since so many people tune in for the game, _____ believe that they get good _____ for their money.

A. Fill in the blanks with the appropriate expressions.

> commercial   competition   stock   statistics   security

1. A _____ guard's responsibility is to protect property, assets, or people.

2. The _____ market has sustained a downward inclination for the last six weeks.

3. Congratulations! You finally made it through despite the stiff _____ .

4. According to _____ , about 20% of the world's population suffers from starvation.

5. We get information about products through magazine advertisements and TV _____ s.

B. Match each expression in column A with the matching expression in column B.

A	B
1. creative •	• tiring
2. rewarding •	• funny
3. fraudulent •	• satisfying
4. strenuous •	• cheating
5. hilarious •	• innovative

C. Fill in the blanks with the appropriate expressions.

1. His artwork, which became extremely popular online, enabled him to make money _____ his website.

2. Julie got involved _____ the plays performed by the drama class that she took after school.

3. To be successful, you should always be prepared to take advantage _____ good opportunities.

4. Here is a list of books that will help you stay motivated and pumped _____ .

5. Many men actually shell _____ a lot of money for the wedding ceremony to satisfy their brides.

D. Fill in the blanks with the appropriate expressions. Use the given words.

1. Find out how to _____ your workspace using our toolbar. (personal)

2. It is essential to exercise regularly and maintain a _____ diet. (balance)

3. Dennis decided to start his own business and become _____ independent. (financial)

4. My _____ comes from poets and novelists. (inspire)

5. There is still an issue whether the _____ cost of space exploration is worth it. (astronomy)

E. Choose the best word to complete each sentence.

1. The qualities for successful leaders include self-confidence, motivation, and
   _____.
   ① detection   ② development   ③ deterioration   ④ determination

2. The committee reported that we have to _____ more in advertising to make a greater profit.
   ① spread   ② alter   ③ modify   ④ invest

3. Whatever he does, he can't _____ us from achieving our goal.
   ① hinder   ② fulfill   ③ protect   ④ take

4. People often _____ Valentine's Day with giving presents or declaring one's love.
   ① assume   ② associate   ③ imagine   ④ believe

5. Time will _____ tell who is responsible for this tragic incident.
   ① creatively   ② financially   ③ ultimately   ④ suddenly

Personal and Demonstrative Pronouns

▌ Why are pronouns important?

You can guess the meaning of the context better by understanding pronouns. Using them, you can avoid using the same word or expressions repeatedly. You can also make sentences easy and clear to understand.

▌ To identity what personal and demonstrative pronouns refer to

- **Step 1**

  Remember. In English, singular and plural should be made clear.
  For singular nouns, singular pronouns such as this/ that/ it are used.
  For plural nouns, plural pronouns such as these/ those/ they are used.

- **Step 2**

  Read the context carefully. Pronouns can refer to preceding words, phrases or even sentences.

- **When a pronoun refer to the preceding word:**

  International Cricket Championship will be held in March. It will be the biggest event in many countries including Britain, New Zealand and Australia.
  What does "it" refer to? – International Cricket Championship

- **When a pronoun refer to the preceding phrase:**

  Your photographs of the earthquake in China took me back to my childhood in Japan. They brought my experience back.
  What does "they" refer to? – Your photographs

- **When a demonstrative pronoun refer to the preceding sentence:**

  A survey by the Mainichi Shimbun found that the president's popularity has dropped by 20%. This means that soon the president would have a difficult time.
  What does "this" refer to? – The fact that the president's popularity has dropped by 20%

Mini Test

What does each demonstrative pronoun refer to?

1. A regular exercise program will improve your overall fitness. It will definitely help you stay healthy.

   → It refers to _____ .

2. If you are under stress, why not take a holiday for a week? This will refresh your mind and it will boost your energy level.

   → This refers to _____ .

3. Last month, Canada proposed adding the polar bear to the list. This will make people aware of the importance of preserving the of environment.

   → This refers to the fact that _____ .

Read the passage. What does each demonstrative pronoun refer to?

4. Are thinking about taking a package holiday for singles? Zebra Tour Agency has arranged a special program, geared to specific groups. If you want to get away from your routines, (a) this will be a good chance. Airfare is based on a return flight from Australia. However, for clients who arrange their own schedule from elsewhere in the world, (b) this is deducted.

   What do (a) and (b) refer to?

   (a) _____ (b) _____

Only those who risk going far can possibly find out how far one can go.
- T. S. Eliot

Unit 5

People

Read the following and answer the questions.

Who is the first promising Asian composer to produce albums for leading US pop singers? In early 2008, a Harvard University publication described a Korean musician in an article. Park Jinyoung, simply known as JYP, produced albums for Will Smith, Mase, and Cassie, which appeared on the Billboard Top 10 Chart.

No one doubts his success as a singer, songwriter and CEO of JYP Entertainment, which is leading Korean pop music. These endeavors have made him one of the most successful entrepreneurs in Asia.

Since debuting in 1994 with his first album Blue City, he has gained a lot of media attention. Unlike other successful musicians, he majored in geology instead of a music related field. Apart from his musical talents, he gained fame for his unique fashion style. In the past, he wore unusual garments like tight shirts, transparent clothing, and bodysuits. This shocking clothing became a controversy among traditionalistic Koreans. In the conservative Korean society, his fashion choices gained him notoriety. However he didn't care about what others thought of him. He crossed over to America to pursue his dream.

Currently, he is producing music for two Asian singers, Min and G-soul, who will debut in America. You might think his success to be just good luck; however, his success is a direct result of his innovative personality.

| Words | Read the following definitions and translate them into Korean. |

- **composer:** a person who creates music _____
- **endeavor:** an attempt to do something, especially something new _____
- **entrepreneur:** a person who organizes and manages their own business _____
- **debut:** to be introduced for the first time _____
- **geology:** a field of science dealing with the physical nature and history of the earth _____
- **controversy:** something that people argue or have different opinions about _____
- **traditionalistic:** sticking to the traditional way of thinking _____
- **conservative:** believing in old values, not modern _____

1. Which saying best describes the writer's attitude towards JYP?

① Lost time is never found.
② You can't have your cake and eat it, too.
③ A penny saved is a penny earned.
④ The grass is always greener on the other side.
⑤ Nothing ventured, nothing gained.

2. Which topic is NOT mentioned about JYP in the passage?

① his producing career
② the genre of music he specializes in
③ his unique fashion style
④ foreign singers he produced albums for
⑤ his educational background

3. Write T if the statement is true. Write F if it is false.

① JYP is the first musician who crossed over to the US. _____
② His university major is not closely related to his current job. _____
③ Blue City is one of the albums which appeared on the Billboard Top 10 Chart. _____

TIP

The Birth of Teenage Idols

+ In Japan and Korea, teenage idols are created by talent agencies. These agencies pick teenage (or sometimes even younger) boys and girls and train them. These kids take voice training, dancing lessons, and even learn foreign languages. Teen idols have great opportunities at an early age, but often lose out on having an ordinary childhood.

Read the following and answer the questions.

Friends support us in good times and bad, and share our joys and sorrows; therefore, we must choose our friends wisely. Surrounding ourselves with those who are loyal, positive, sympathetic and loving is the obvious choice, however, some still make the mistake of letting friend-enemies, also known as 'frienemies,' into their circle. So who are these toxic friends?

One is the drama-queen. This type of person can't lead a calm life because they are forever involved in one crisis after the next in order to generate attention for themselves. Although entertaining, drama queens treat their friends as personal counselors using them to help clean up their own disasters.

People should also avoid those who are manipulative and power-hungry, like the control freak. This type will stop at nothing to make their friends feel inferior, and (a) _____ (significant) so that they can control them. If you surround yourself with control freaks it will be difficult to build healthy self-esteem.

As the saying, (b) '_____ _____' insinuates, people usually befriend those who have common interests and personalities. Therefore, be careful when choosing friends. Not only will they influence the enjoyment you get out of life, they will also be a reflection of who you are as a person.

| Words | Read the following definitions and translate them into Korean. |

- **sympathetic:** relating to the condition of others _____
- **generate:** to cause something to begin or to develop _____
- **manipulative:** persuasive in a controlling way _____
- **insignificant:** unimportant _____
- **self-esteem:** how one views their self worth _____
- **insinuate:** to imply or suggest something _____
- **befriend:** to make friends with _____

1. Which is the most appropriate saying for the blank (b)?

① Like father, like son.
② Two heads are better than one.
③ Birds of a feather flock together.
④ Friend in need is a friend indeed.
⑤ There is no rose without a thorn.

Speed Reading

2. What is the most appropriate expression for the blank (a)?
Use the given word.

_____

3. Match the main idea with each paragraph.

Paragraph 1 •   • Advice on avoiding people who
                          constantly cause dramatic situations

Paragraph 2 •   • Advice on choosing positive friends

Paragraph 3 •   • Advice on avoiding people who are
                          controlling and manipulative

TIP

What People Say About Friendship...

- A friend in need is a friend indeed: A true friend is someone who helps you when you are in trouble.
- A man is known by the company he keeps: A person's character is judged by the type of people with whom they spend their time.
- Better to be alone than in bad company: Be careful when choosing the people you associate with.
- False friends are worse than open enemies: Friends who don't have your best interests in mind are just as bad as enemies.

Read the following and answer the questions.

"The heaven of fakes" is one of many nicknames attributed to China. Whether it is a $100 Chanel bag, or a $5 new release DVD, there is nothing you cannot find a replica of. The latest fake item in China is a take on *Harry Potter*, the best selling series written by J.K. Rowling.

According to the NY Times, at least a dozen unauthorized *Harry Potter* titles are sold on the street corners, and even more on websites. However, at least one author of <u>fake</u> *Harry Potter* books shares the same intention as J.K. Rowling: giving dreams and fantasies to children.

Li Jingsheng, a manager at a Shanghai textile factory, is the author of the phony story of *Harry Potter*, titled, "*Harry Potter and the Showdown*." His son kept asking him what would happen to the story after *Harry Potter 6*, so Mr. Li decided to write his own version of *Harry Potter* for his son. As a high school graduate factory manager, it was not easy to write a story to impress his son who had already read the real *Harry Potter*. He had to wake up early and go to bed late to create the 250,000-word novel.

Despite the disregard for copyright law, we have to applaud the effort of this father who spent all his free time writing a story to please his son. Although creating a fake *Harry Potter* story is illegal, his love toward his son is genuine.

| Words | Read the following definitions and translate them into Korean. |

- **fake:** an imitated thing _____
- **unauthorized:** not legally allowed to do something _____
- **phony:** fake, _____
- **version:** something that tells in one's own words _____
- **disregard:** neglect of something _____
- **applaud:** to congratulate, to give recognition to _____
- **genuine:** true, real _____

1. Which best describes the writer's attitude towards the fake
   Harry Potter series?

   ① Negative
   ② Understanding
   ③ Unclear
   ④ Critical
   ⑤ Fully supportive

2. Which best describes the writer's opinion?

   ① Unconditional love from parents can be dangerous.
   ② Copyright laws should be flexible.
   ③ The Chinese government should crack down on fake items.
   ④ Phony *Harry Potter* books can be an expression of parental love.
   ⑤ The original version of the *Harry Potter* series should be more
      valued than fake ones.

Speed Reading

3. Which word has the opposite meaning of the underlined part?
   Find the word in the passage.

   _____

 TIP

Right or Left?

+ Have you heard the term 'copyleft?' It is a movement against strict copyright laws.
  However, it is not the same as copyright piracy. Copyright laws give authors the
  right to prohibit others from reproducing or adapting their work. While copyright
  only protects the originator's rights, copyleft gives users the freedom to improve
  or adapt the work of others.

Read the following and answer the questions.

Who do you think was the world's richest man from 1995 to 2007? How about Harvard's most successful dropout and the founder of Microsoft? Bingo! It's Bill Gates. Do you know that he is also a well-known founder of many charities? Every year Bill Gates donates millions of dollars out of his own pocket to various charities.

He set up the Bill & Melinda Gates Foundation in 2000, where he and his family donated huge amounts of money to many non-profit organizations and scientific research programs. He established this foundation with two simple values in mind. First, "all lives — no matter where they are being lived — have equal value." Second, (a) "to whom much is given, much is expected." These two beliefs were the driving force behind his generous donations to charity.

Through his foundation, he and his family sponsor various global health programs. He is involved in programs to benefit child health, AIDS, malaria, poor nutrition, and tuberculosis in underdeveloped countries. The foundation also provides (b) grants to poor but promising students and scholars. He aids the students through scholarship programs such as the Gates Cambridge Scholarship and the Gates Millennium Scholarship.

His wealth was estimated at over $58 billion in 2008. Bill Gates continues to take generous philanthropic initiatives in the areas that have been neglected or unnoticed by governments and organizations. It's truly astonishing to see how one individual can make such a huge difference.

| Words | Read the following definitions and translate them into Korean. |

- **dropout**: a person who withdraws from school before graduating _____
- **donate**: to give money to a cause _____
- **non-profit**: not intended to earn a profit (gain, benefit) _____
- **nutrition**: anything that nourishes, nourishment, food _____
- **estimate**: to calculate approximately _____
- **initiative**: the action of taking the first step or move _____

1. Which is the main theme of the passage?

① Bill Gates as a philanthropist
② Bill Gates as the most successful person
③ Bill Gates as the wealthiest person
④ How a person can change the world
⑤ Why more organizations should be founded

2. Which does the underlined part (a) imply?

① You have to give back what you've received from society.
② Wealthy people tend to donate a lot.
③ You have to think twice about who you are.
④ Don't expect too much from society.
⑤ Hard working is the key to being wealthy.

Speed Reading
3. Which is the closest in meaning to the underlined part (b)?

① to give someone a prize
② to allow someone to have something
③ to accept and agree that something is true
④ a reward for doing good work
⑤ an amount of money that a government gives to an individual

TIP

Wishes Do Come True

✦ The Make-a-Wish Foundation is the name of the international non-profit organization that make wishes come true for children who have life-threatening illnesses. Of course, the people who work for the foundation are not fairy godmothers, so they can't grant impossible wishes. However, if a child wanted to meet his idol, for example, it could be made possible. In 2008, Minseung, a 9-year-old boy who suffers from Leukemia, met his superstar, soccer player David Beckham.

Read the following and answer the questions.

The year 2008 could be a historic moment in the United States. Many Americans are overjoyed at the possibility that the first African-American president might be elected.

Barack Obama, the United States Senator and presidential candidate, could very well make the whole nation excited. African-Americans have been long overdue to have someone of their own race represent them in the highest government position in their nation.

Born to a Kenyan father and an American mother, Obama's childhood was not a happy one. His father was the college's first African student and his mother was Caucasian. Unfortunately, their marriage ended in divorce and Obama's mother had to raise him by herself.

As a "free-spirited" woman with strong determination, she raised her son with _____. When they lived in Indonesia, she used to wake Obama up at 4 a.m. for English lessons.

She also worked for Women's World Banking and for the U.S. Agency for International Development. His mother's work in the international world must have certainly impressed and influenced him.

When asked about his most precious memento, Barack Obama didn't hesitate to reply, "I value a photograph of the cliffs of the South Shore of Oahu in Hawaii, where my mother's ashes were scattered." In his biography, he also confessed, "I know that she was the kindest, most generous spirit I have ever known, and that what is best in me I owe to her."

He was right. His mother never failed to inspire and encourage him to push on and move upwards. The lessons he learned from his mother, such as honesty, free judgment, and dreams, definitely made him what he is now.

1. **Which is the most appropriate headline for the article?**

   ① Who Can Work for the World?
   ② Why Are Americans Waiting for a New President?
   ③ What's Behind the Historical Figure, Barrack Obama? .
   ④ How Can We Change the Future of a Child?
   ⑤ How Can One's Life Be Affected by His or Her Childhood?

2. **Which is the most appropriate expression for the blank?**

   ① honesty
   ② strict regulations
   ③ generosity
   ④ free spirit
   ⑤ self-regulation

3. **Complete the summary by filling in the blanks with the given expressions. Change the form, if necessary.**

   | attribute | African-American | upbringing | frontrunner | despite |

   _____ an unhappy childhood, Barack Obama has worked his way up to being a(n) _____ in the 2008 US elections. He could very well be the first _____ president of the United States. When asked, Obama _____ success to the _____ he received from his mother.

   Words   Read the following definitions and find the words in the passage.

   • a member of a senate, the upper house of the legislature of the U.S.: _____
   • a person who seeks an office or award: _____
   • open-minded: _____
   • something kept in memory of the giver or an event: _____
   • to think highly of: _____
   • a story of a person's life: _____
   • to admit or say something: _____

A. Fill in the blanks with the appropriate expressions.

> estimate   controversy   trustworthy   donate   endeavor

1. Nick's _____ to help his brother to pass the exam was in vain.
2. If I were Mike, I would not tell any secrets to Susan. She is not _____.
3. If I were rich, I would _____ to aid hungry children in Africa.
4. John's latest book gave rise to a lot of _____ .
5. Before you leave, try to _____ how long your trip will take.

B. Connect each expression in column A with the matching expression in column B.

A	B
1. insinuate •	• conservative
2. insignificant •	• unimportant
3. traditionalistic •	• imply

C. Fill in the blanks with the appropriate expressions.

> apart from   in the long run   despite   according to   make a difference

1. If you would exercise half an hour a day, it can _____ to your health.
2. _____ yourself, does anybody else support your plan?
3. _____ her hard work, she was not able to pass the exam.
4. If she pays off her debt, it will benefit her _____ .
5. _____ the professor, there will be major changes in the schedule.

D. Fill in the blanks with the appropriate expressions. Use the given words.

1. You had better _____ to your lies before your parents figure it out.
   (confess)

2. My music teacher was _____ to students without musical talent.
   (sympathy)

3. Some Chinese goods are _____ for their poor quality. (notoriety)

4. Lack of food is not a(n) _____ problem to children in North Korea.
   (insignificance)

5. _____ for education comes from the central government. (financial)

E. Choose the best word to complete each sentence.

1. Old people are usually more _____ than the young as they pay attention to
   tradition.
   ① ambitious   ② conservative   ③ appealing   ④ confident

2. Meat, vegetable, and milk provide an important source of _____ for
   the human body.
   ① pressure   ② entertainment   ③ nutrition   ④ balance

3. Frank Lloyd Wright was a(n) _____ architect who designed many modern
   and avant-garde buildings.
   ① technical   ② arrogant   ③ innovative   ④ careful

4. If you want to be a leader, you should use your own _____ . Do not wait for
   somebody else to tell you what to do.
   ① initiative   ② achievement   ③ attention   ④ support

Using Context Clues to Guess Word Meanings

Why are context clues important?

You can guess the meaning of words that you do not know by using the context clues. Plus, it makes reading comprehension faster. Using context clues, you can skip over the unknown word completely.

How to guess the meaning of a word using Context Clues

- **Step 1**

  Decide whether you need to know the meaning of a word to understand the writing. If you do, guess the meaning from context. If not, skip the word.

- **Step 2**

  Imagine that there is a blank line there. Then substitute a word that you know in the space. This word will probably be similar in meaning to the word that you don't know.

Types of context clues

1. Synonym

   A word that has the same meaning can be guessed from the context
   - Many U.S. companies are downsizing — or reducing the number of employees — in order to save money and increase the amount of profit that they can make.
   - Sports are universal, and very few people have not succumbed, or given in, to their lure at one time or another.

2. Antonym

   A word or group of words that has the opposite meaning can be guessed from the context.
   - Although some men are loquacious, others hardly talk at all.
   - I expected my family to be ecstatic to see me, but they were very angry that I'd left school without permission.

Mini Test

Find the expression that is similar to each bolded word.

1. Jackie was filled with **mortification** because of her careless remark.

   ① proud   ② shame   ③ confident   ④ happy

2. His **rancor** of his brother has caused him to live his life as a lonely person.

   ① love   ② generous   ③ tolerance   ④ hatred

3. The events for the conference were listed in **chronological** order. They began with
   the first event of the day and ended with the closing ceremonies in the evening.

   ① out of order   ② broken   ③ messed up   ④ in order of occurrence

Find the expression that is opposite of each bolded word.

4. Instead of living in the city with other people, she chose to be a **recluse**.

   ① vegetarian   ② one who lives alone
   ③ teacher   ④ government leader

5. The librarian instructed us to use hushed voices, unlike the **raucous** sounds
   we'd made in gym class.

   ① loud   ② happy   ③ angry   ④ serious

6. Louisa's organized clear speech was well prepared, unlike Tara's presentation
   which was **inarticulate**.

   ① entertaining   ② persuasive   ③ unclear   ④ brief

MEMO

MEMO